A GREATER than Solomon

by G. Christian Weiss
Voice of Missions
Back to the Bible Broadcast

A
BACK TO THE BIBLE
PUBLICATION

Back to the Bible
Lincoln, Nebraska 68501

88,000 printed to date—1978
(5-7845—4M—98)
ISBN 0-8474-1207-5

Printed in the United States of America

Foreword

The Old Testament furnishes us with the history of a number of persons who are types of Christ. Being types, they are, of course, but shadowy outlines of Him who "is the radiance of His glory and the exact representation of His nature, and upholds all things by the word of His power" (Heb. 1:3, NASB).

This book, *A Greater Than Solomon*, traces the Person and work of Christ as dimly prefigured in Solomon and his reign. By a series of contrasts the author shows how infinitely superior is the Lord of glory to Israel's king who ruled his nation at the zenith of its power and material wealth.

After reading this stimulating, Christ-centered series of radio messages given over the overseas network of the Back to the Bible Broadcast, the words of the hymn by Robert Grant come to mind:

> O worship the King, all glorious above,
>   O gratefully sing His power and His love;
> Our Shield and Defender, the Ancient of Days,
>   Pavilioned in splendor and girded with praise.
>
> Frail children of dust, and feeble as frail,
>   In Thee do we trust, nor find Thee to fail;
> Thy mercies how tender! how firm to the end!
>   Our Maker, Defender, Redeemer and Friend.

—The Publishers

Contents

Chapter 1

The True Measure of Greatness

On several occasions Jesus' disciples argued which of them should be the greatest. This seems to us to be an unfitting topic for men who had walked and talked with Jesus for three years, but it reveals a trait of human nature. It is a mark of carnality, one altogether too common among Christians. The desire for greatness has plagued humanity ever since the fall of Adam. It is a plague in people and among nations and in human institutions. Many wars of history have been fought over the issue of who should be the greatest.

The desire for greatness lurks by nature within everyone. But the regenerating, sanctifying work of the Holy Spirit should uproot it from the Christian's heart. At least it should not dominate his life. Yet many Christians' lives seem to be ruled by just such a desire.

"And he came to Capernaum: and being in the house he asked them, What was it that ye disputed among yourselves by the way? But they held their peace: for by the way they had disputed among themselves, who should be the greatest. And he sat down, and called the twelve, and saith unto them, If any man desire to be first, the same shall be last of all, and servant of all. And he took a child, and set him in the midst of them: and when he had taken him in his arms, he said unto them, Whosoever shall receive one of such children in my name, receiveth me" (Mark 9:33-37).

Some of the disciples may have answered the call of Christ in the first place because of a desire for greatness. Believing that He was the Messiah and that He would set up His kingdom, they may have thought that by forsaking their humble professions to follow Him, they would almost surely be given some exalted place in His messianic kingdom. Instead of being peasants, they would become princes. Instead of being fishermen, they hoped to be rulers. They supposed that they would be in on the ground floor by answering His call to discipleship. This is a very wrong motive for Christian discipleship. But were those disciples the only ones guilty of this? Is not the desire for advancement and aggression a motive that dominates many Christian disciples today—even Christian ministers?

But while these disciples sought after greatness, they did not really know what true greatness was. Jesus propounded an interpretation very different from their own. His definition of greatness is far removed from every human definition or conception of greatness.

There are three common estimates of greatness in the world:

First, there is the childish view—that greatness consists simply in having an abundance of material things. The more things a person has, the greater and more important that person is. Though it is a childish estimate, it is a very common one. Multitudes of people in the world judge human greatness by a person's bank account and the material possessions he has been able to accumulate. Whenever the question "How much is he worth?" is asked, it invariably means "How much money does he have?"

This conception has entered into Christian thinking too. More often than not when a pastor says of a certain individual, "He is one of my leading members," he means the man is a bank president or a wealthy businessman or perhaps the head of a corporation.

Second, the barbarian estimate says that greatness is might, or force. Primitive men have always judged a man's greatness by his sheer strength and have slaughtered one another to prove their superiority. It is really a jungle idea. But though barbarian and primitive, this idea is very common even today. In the highest echelons of human society this barbarian estimate of greatness still persists. It is true of individuals, and it is also true of nations. A man is a "great hero" because he is huge and able to knock out his opponent in the boxing ring. A football player is a "great player" because he is big and powerful and by sheer, brute strength can overcome his opponents, even if it brings injury to some of them. A man is judged "great" if he is able to ruthlessly override all opposers and go straight to the top, regardless of how many men may be hurt along the way.

Nations are judged great if they have superior military force. The more power of destruction a nation has, the greater it is; the greater its armies, the greater its navies, the greater its instruments of destruction, the greater the nation. National greatness is invariably judged on the ground of military might rather than moral strength and spiritual quality.

Third, the Greek estimate of greatness is intellect. The ancient Greeks worshiped intellectual attainment and knowledge. Their great men were their philosophers and teachers. In fact, the ancient Greek philosopher set a standard of greatness on the basis of intellectual attainment that has persisted through all succeeding generations. Even the Scriptures testify, "The Greeks seek after wisdom" (I Cor. 1:22). They revered and idolized intellectual greatness. Yet their civilization, like all other civilizations, collapsed, for it sought to attain greatness by false, human standards rather than by true, divine standards.

The ancient Greek estimate is a common conception today. This is the day of education and intellectualism. A man is great because he has a Ph.D. and because he heads up an important department in a famous university. He carries influence among others because he is learned and intellectual. He is so great in the eyes of people that his influence can turn them away from God if that is the set of his own sails. While education can be a great asset to a man, mere education is no sign of true greatness. In fact, intellectual people can be, and often are, very "little" people in actuality.

These then are man's standards of greatness—bank accounts, biceps and brains. Almost all human beings are judged great in the eyes of their fellowmen by one or more of these three erroneous standards.

The concept of being great by any one of these three human standards has been a barrier and stumbling block in the lives and spiritual development of Christian people. This is the thing that has kept people from dedication to God's service. It has kept young people from the mission fields. It has kept men called of God from entering the Christian ministry. It has deterred multitudes of Christians from fulfilling the will of God. Lurking in their being was the desire to be great, and wrong conceptions of greatness led them in wrong directions.

A suave businessman entered the lobby of a metropolitan hotel where Dr. George Washington Carver was quietly sitting in an alcove not far from the registration desk. The businessman brusquely motioned to Dr. Carver to come and carry his bags to his room, thinking he was a bellhop. Dr. Carver humbly obliged by carrying the heavy bags on to the elevator, accompanying the gentleman to his floor and then depositing the bags in his room. When he was offered a tip, Carver, of course, declined. A bit nonplussed, the man inquired into the reason for the decline of the tip.

"I do not work here," Dr. Carver said. "I am not a regular bellboy."

The man then wanted to know just who he was. When Dr. Carver gave his name, he exclaimed, "Not George Washington Carver, the famous scientist!"

"Yes," replied Dr. Carver, "I am George Washington Carver, the scientist to whom you refer."

"But why did you carry my bags for me?" the man asked.

"Oh, I was very happy to serve you, Sir," quietly replied Dr. Carver.

Who was really the "great" man of the two? I cannot tell you the name of that businessman, and I doubt if anyone else could, but people all over the world know the name of Dr. George Washington Carver—naturalist, scientist and Christian.

James Hudson Taylor was a physician. When he announced his decision to go as a missionary to China, a brother apparently thought him little short of being a fool. The brother chose a political career and ultimately became a member of the British parliament. A certain British encyclopedia gave quite a respectable account of the life and labors of J. Hudson Taylor, the missionary; but its terse statement following the politician brother's name and birth and death dates was simply "A brother of J. Hudson Taylor."

God rejects man's estimates of greatness and sets them completely aside. What is His standard of greatness? His Son, Jesus Christ, our Lord and Saviour, gave us three standards:

First, by God's standard greatness involves service. To His jealous, bickering disciples, Jesus solemnly said, "If any man desire to be first, the same shall be last of all, and servant of all" (Mark 9:35). How radically different this concept was! There was no "big shot" concept with Jesus Christ. This was the idea which His disciples held, but He quickly dissipated it. George Washington Carver demonstrated Jesus' interpretation of greatness when he gave to the businessman his reason for carrying his bags: "I was very happy to serve you, Sir."

Greatness does not consist in attaining a status of wealth and prominence where, instead of finding it necessary to serve, one is served by others. Though this is the world's estimate, it is not God's. Few men, even unbelievers, would argue that Jesus was the greatest Man who ever lived. But let us not forget that He said, "The Son of man came not to be ministered unto, but to minister, and to give his life a ransom for many" (Matt. 20:28). In the upper room that last night with His disciples He girded Himself with a towel and knelt down to wash their feet. Then He said to them, "Ye call me Master and Lord: and ye say well; for so I am. If I then, your Lord and Master, have washed your feet; ye also ought to wash one another's feet" (John 13:13,14).

Second, the divine estimate of greatness involves sacrifice. In the chapter of Mark's Gospel immediately preceding the one from which our text is taken, we read that Jesus said to His disciples, "Whosoever will come after me, let him deny himself, and take up his cross, and follow me. For whosoever will save his life shall lose it; but whosoever shall lose his life for my sake and the gospel's, the same shall save it" (8:34,35).

These disciples were not yet "great" disciples, because they had not yet come to the place where they were willing to sacrifice themselves. They were not willing to lose their lives for His sake or the gospel's or for any other external cause. Yet, the world's greatest heroes, after all, are the ones who have made the greatest sacrifices for the sake of others. Hudson Taylor is recognized as a great man even in the annals of world history, and he was a man of great sacrifice. His name stands out in the annals of Christian missions. He "threw his life away" in the interior of China for Christ's sake and the gospel's, and he "saved" his life by doing it. This is true greatness.

William Carey "sacrificed" his life and everything he had to take the gospel to India. He endured great hardships and encountered suffering. At first it seemed that he was surely wasting his life, but today William Carey is reckoned a great man, known and revered everywhere as the father of modern missions. Some of the greatest men I have ever known are missionaries who have sacrificed their all for the sake of Christ and the gospel.

Third, the divine standard of greatness involves self-denial. Jesus said, "Whosoever will come after me, let him deny himself, and take up his cross, and follow me" (v. 34).

The disciples had no such conception as this. When Jesus spoke to them about His own crucifixion, Simon Peter responded by saying, "Be it far from thee, Lord" (Matt. 16:22). And Jesus replied, "Get thee behind me, Satan: thou art an offence unto me: for thou savourest not the things that be of God, but those that be of men" (v. 23). Simon Peter did not like the thought of self-denial, of a cross, of death, of suffering. And yet he wanted to "come after" Jesus. He wanted to be a disciple of the Lord; he wanted indeed to be a "great" disciple, but he had the wrong conception of greatness.

In the kingdom of God the way up is down— always. Simon Peter ultimately learned this. In his epistle he wrote: "Yea, all of you be subject one to another, and be clothed with humility: for God resisteth the proud, and giveth grace to the humble. Humble yourselves therefore under the mighty hand of God, that he may exalt you in due time" (I Pet. 5:5,6).

The Apostle James added his testimony: "Humble yourselves in the sight of the Lord, and he shall lift you up" (James 4:10). James became one of the great "pillars" of the early Church, but he, too, had learned that the way up was down. Along with Simon Peter, he had learned that "God

14

resisteth the proud, and giveth grace to the humble" (I Pet. 5:5).

The world may cry, "Fool," to the man who takes a humble place in life, but in the end all must recognize that humility is greatness, that self-denial is exaltation, and that the way up is down.

God needs some "great" men these days for His work. The needs of the world now demand great missionaries, great men and women, a whole host of them. It appears to be God's present plan that such people volunteer for the service of Christ, but these will have to be people who are great—not by carnal standards, but by divine standards.

Chapter 2

Greater Than Solomon in Wisdom

"The queen of the south shall rise up in the judgment with this generation, and shall condemn it: for she came from the uttermost parts of the earth to hear the wisdom of Solomon; and, behold, a greater than Solomon is here" (Matt. 12:42).

History centers largely in great men and is woven around their characters and exploits. The greatest man in history is Jesus Christ. He stands out in bold relief above, and in contrast to, all others. In fact, history has been called "His-story," and it is to a very large extent, especially certain areas of history.

With sublime dignity Jesus compared Himself to the greatest men of earth and without hesitation or arrogance said, "A greater than these is here." Comparing Himself with the famous Prophet Jonah, He said, "A greater than Jonas is here" (Matt. 12:41). And then, referring to the great and renowned King Solomon, He said again, "Behold, a greater than Solomon is here" (v. 42). In referring to Himself in such a way He manifested not pride, not vanity, but a sublime awareness of His true position—a holy dignity of deity.

By comparing Himself with Solomon He was drawing a high comparison indeed, as far as worldly standards are concerned, for Solomon was a great man by almost every such standard. He was held in exceedingly high esteem by the nation of Israel from his own time right up to the time of Christ and even today. Solomon, in fact, is esteemed and honored by people around the whole world to this present day. He is depicted in the Bible as being a very great person, but Jesus Christ is "greater than Solomon." We shall consider the various aspects in which this is seen to be true.

Jesus exceeded Solomon in wisdom. King Solomon was noted, almost above all else, for his vast wisdom. It was perhaps the most outstanding of all his remarkable qualities. The Queen of Sheba, Jesus reminded His hearers, came from the uttermost part of the earth to investigate the wisdom of Solomon, and then Christ boldly added, "Behold, a greater than Solomon is here" (v. 42). Though the Queen of Sheba had come from a distant land to hear wisdom from Solomon, He, the Son of God, was in their midst with greater wisdom than that of their renowned hero, and they would not listen to Him. So the Queen of Sheba and the people of her generation would rise up in judgment against the people among whom He stood as He spoke these words.

The entire context of Jesus' words concerns the admiration this queen showed toward Solomon's superb wisdom. She had heard of his unusual wisdom even though she lived in a distant land (perhaps in northeastern Africa), and she came "to prove" him with "hard questions," to test his wisdom. She was convinced by what she found. In fact, she was so impressed that she said to Solomon, "The half was not told me." Among other things she exclaimed: "Happy are thy men, happy are these thy servants, which stand continually before thee, and that hear thy wisdom!" (I Kings 10:8).

We are also told that this wealthy queen gave Solomon "an hundred and twenty talents of gold, and of spices very great store, and precious stones" (v. 10). These gifts may have totaled $25 million or more in American money. She gave all these things because she was profoundly affected by the king's wisdom and knowledge.

She seemed to recognize and acknowledge that Solomon had been given this wisdom from God. It had, indeed, been given to him in answer to prayer at the very beginning of his reign: "The Lord appeared to Solomon in a dream by night: and God said, Ask what I shall give thee. And Solomon said, . . . Give therefore thy servant an understanding heart to judge thy people" (I Kings 3:5,6,9). Instead of asking for long life or riches or honor, Solomon asked God for understanding and practical wisdom in order that he might wisely rule his people. His request pleased God and also inspired the confidence of his people. The wisdom which he manifested at the very outset of his reign in judging between two mothers and a child (see vv. 16-27) from village to village throughout the entire country: "And all Israel heard of the judgment which the king had judged; and they feared the king: for they saw that the wisdom of God was in him" (v. 28).

Solomon wrote the books in the Old Testament that are commonly known as "The Books of Wisdom." It was he who wrote Proverbs, Ecclesiastes and the Song of Solomon. Proverbs and Ecclesiastes particularly are books of wisdom. I think they contain the most profound, and at the same

18

time most practical, wisdom ever put into writing.

We are told that Solomon "spake three thousand proverbs: and his songs were a thousand and five. And he spake of trees, from the cedar tree that is in Lebanon even unto the hyssop that springeth out of the wall: he spake also of beasts, and of fowl, and of creeping things, and of fishes" (I Kings 4:32,33). The Book of Proverbs contains 915 verses, but the Book of First Kings states that Solomon uttered 3000 proverbs. So the entire Book of Proverbs contains less than one-third of all the proverbs spoken by this wise king. His wisdom embraced the entire realm of nature and much relating to the spirit of man and eternal things.

In the Book of Ecclesiastes he himself testified: "I gave my heart to seek and search out by wisdom concerning all things that are done under heaven" (Eccles. 1:13); "I gave my heart to know wisdom" (v. 17). He could honestly say, "I . . . have gotten more wisdom than all they that have been before me in Jerusalem: yea, my heart had great experience of wisdom and knowledge" (v. 16).

The Bible unequivocally states, "Solomon's wisdom excelled the wisdom of all the children of the east country, and all the wisdom of Egypt. For he was wiser than all men: . . . and his fame was in all nations round about" (I Kings 4:30,31). The ancient seers of the East were noted for their wisdom. The early Egyptians also possessed remarkable knowledge and understanding and were skilled in many arts and sciences. We marvel today at the knowledge these people possessed as evidenced by the things which they achieved and built on the earth, but Solomon's wisdom was exceptional. He was wiser than all others combined. The Bible says,

"And there came of all people to hear the wisdom of Solomon, from the kings of the earth, which had heard of his wisdom" (v. 34). He is ranked among earth's greatest men and is known universally as the wisest man who ever lived, and yet Jesus Christ is greater in wisdom than Solomon.

Solomon, though wise, nevertheless manifested deficiencies in wisdom. By his own confession some things were too hard for him to understand. In the Book of Ecclesiastes Solomon made this statement: "When I applied mine heart to know wisdom, and to see the business that is done upon the earth: (for also there is that neither day nor night seeth sleep with his eyes:) then I beheld all the work of God, that a man cannot find out the work that is done under the sun: because . . . though a wise man think to know it, yet shall he not be able to find it" (Eccles. 8:16; see 7:23). This is the testimony of the great and wise Solomon. He stated that there are many things done upon earth, both by men and God, which no one can understand. Though he had given his heart to seek out wisdom and knowledge, and though he had more knowledge than all other men of the earth, yet he confessed that man simply cannot know some things. So his knowledge was confessedly deficient.

Jesus, on the other hand, was never nonplussed for lack of wisdom and never devoid of the answer to any hard question. Though His enemies repeatedly tried to trip Him with calculated trick questions, He was able on every occasion to give the right answer. They were amazed and dumbfounded.

20

Solomon was a strange combination of both wisdom and folly, but Jesus never manifested folly. Solomon was inordinately extravagant, self-indulgent and prodigal. We are told in First Kings that every day in his kitchen he utilized 120 bushels of fine flour, 240 bushels of meal, 30 oxen, 100 sheep, plus additional wild game, for he fed at his tables regularly anywhere from 5000 to 10,000 people—officers, servants, dependents and guests. He sat on a throne of solid ivory in an immense and costly palace. His drinking vessels were all of solid gold, as were the vessels of his entire house. This was unnecessary and extravagant.

Solomon also acted foolishly in disobeying the command of God, a very plain command—he married many heathen women. We are told: "Solomon loved many strange women, together with the daughter of Pharaoh, women of the Moabites, Ammonites, Edomites, Zidonians, and Hittites; of the nations concerning which the Lord said unto the children of Israel, Ye shall not go in to them, neither shall they come in unto you: for surely they will turn away your heart after their gods: Solomon clave unto these in love. . . . Solomon did evil in the sight of the Lord, and went not fully after the Lord, as did David his father" (I Kings 11:1,2,6). How utterly foolish this was, especially for so great and wise a man as King Solomon.

With all of his wisdom he was, nevertheless, a very sensual man and became in some respects a senseless man. "He had seven hundred wives, princesses, and three hundred concubines" (v. 3). A thousand women! This was ridiculous and extremely foolish by any standard of prudence.

He was also very foolish in allowing his heathen

wives to worship their pagan idols right in his own palace, setting up altars for them. Worse than that, these heathen women so effectively "turned away his heart" (v. 3) that he participated in their idol worship himself even though he knew the One and only true God. What a strange combination of wisdom and folly is seen in this man!

King Solomon oppressed his people inordinately with heavy taxation to pay for all his excesses. After his death some of the old men of the kingdom said to his son, "Thy father made our yoke grievous: now therefore make thou the grievous service of thy father, and his heavy yoke which he put upon us, lighter, and we will serve thee" (12:4).

Jesus Christ, however, stands flawless in both His wisdom and His character. No such flaws existed in Him or were attributed to Him. With sublime assurance He could ask, "Which of you convinceth me of sin?" (John 8:46). In contrast to Solomon He lived in utter simplicity and always identified Himself with the common people in their daily lives and in their trials and needs.

There was no moral taint on Jesus or even the suggestion of a scandal about Him. He loved all people and especially championed the cause of the oppressed, instead of oppressing as did Solomon. The Bible says of Him, "In whom are hid all the treasures of wisdom and knowledge" (Col. 2:3), and He has been "made unto us wisdom, and righteousness, and sanctification, and redemption" (I Cor. 1:30). He is described as being "the power of God, and the wisdom of God" (v. 24).

Jesus never lacked wisdom for any occasion. Nothing could be hidden from His knowledge. He even knew what was in people's hearts and needed no one to tell Him. Solomon could answer the hard questions put to him by the Queen of Sheba, but Jesus Christ can answer the heart questions of anyone who asks. He knows the heart; He knows its hunger, its need. He knows all the perplexing problems of human life, and He can fully answer and satisfy all the heart questions.

There is a vast difference between the "hard questions" answered by Solomon and the "heart questions" to which Jesus Christ can give answers. He alone can answer the questions of your heart and the problems of your life. He knows all about you; He knows you thoroughly. Nothing in your heart, mind, soul or life is hidden from His all-sufficient wisdom and grace. He knows your every need, and He knows the deepest longings and desires of your being. You, like all others who are descendants of the man who was created in the image and likeness of God, are so made that you cannot find satisfaction apart from Him and true fellowship with Him.

Though Satan tempts men into believing they will find satisfaction in a life of sin and pleasure in disobeying God, this can never be the case. True joy, true satisfaction and true delight are found in reconciliation with God and in walking in fellowship with His Son, Jesus Christ. He and He alone knows the needs and longings of our hearts. If you have never trusted Christ as your Saviour, take advantage of the fact that Christ alone can answer all the inner questions and longings of your heart and reconcile you to God if you will but come to Him in sincerity and truth. Confess that you are one of the sinners for whom He died, and ask Him to be

your Saviour. In Him you will find all the treasures
of wisdom and grace and mercy and peace and joy.

Chapter 3

Greater Than Solomon in Wealth

"The queen of the south shall rise up in the judgment with the men of this generation, and condemn them: for she came from the utmost parts of the earth to hear the wisdom of Solomon; and, behold, a greater than Solomon is here" (Luke 11:31). These words are almost identical to those found in the 12th chapter of the Gospel of Matthew, which we have previously noted. With sublime dignity Jesus compared Himself to the Prophet Jonah and to King Solomon, declaring without hesitation that He is greater than both of them.

We have noted that Solomon was preeminently a man of wisdom, being commonly regarded as the wisest of men on this earth. In comparison we pointed out that Jesus Christ has far greater and more perfect wisdom than Solomon. But Solomon was not noted for his wisdom alone. Other outstanding qualities and characteristics have made him great in history. One noteworthy thing was his astounding wealth.

Solomon was one of the wealthiest men of history and was among the wealthiest of all the earth's kings and rulers. Let us reflect briefly upon the great wealth of this man so that in comparison we may understand how vastly greater are the riches of Jesus Christ, which far exceed all the treasures of Solomon.

The Bible gives a full description of the wealth of King Solomon: "King Solomon made a navy of ships in Eziongeber, which is beside Eloth, on the shore of the Red sea, in the land of Edom. And Hiram sent in the navy his servants, shipmen that had knowledge of the sea, with the servants of Solomon. And they came to Ophir, and fetched from thence gold, four hundred and twenty talents, and brought it to king Solomon" (I Kings 9:26-28).

Every year Solomon received from Hiram this huge amount of gold in tribute, more than $90 million (U.S.) in value at the late-70's rate of $200-plus per troy ounce. This gives us some insight into his fabulous wealth. He had silver from the mines of Asia Minor and perhaps Spain. He had a limitless store of precious stones from various parts of the world, even from the most distant spots. He was rich in all manner of spices, always a prized commodity in the East. He had a great abundance of ivory brought from India and East Africa. His personal throne was made entirely of ivory. Cedar, the most valued wood for building, was brought to him in tremendous quantities from the mountains of Lebanon. He built a temple in Jerusalem, the entire sanctuary of which was covered with pure gold as though it had been carved from one solid mass of gold.

The king himself lived in an exceedingly magnificent palace, lavished with an almost incomprehensible amount of gold, silver, brass and other valuable metals. He ate and drank from vessels of solid gold. He possessed an endless array of servants, domestic as well as imported, and they were all gorgeously arrayed in the most costly clothing.

26

He himself wore more gorgeous apparel than any other king anywhere in the world. His officers, too, were all clad in the most costly uniforms. Wealth was no consideration with King Solomon.

His table was both rich and immense. We are told: "Solomon's provision for one day was thirty measures of fine flour, and threescore measures of meal, ten fat oxen, and twenty oxen out of the pastures, and an hundred sheep, besides harts, and roebucks, and fallowdeer, and fatted fowl" (4:22,23). The "measure" referred to here approximates four of our bushels, meaning that Solomon's provision for each day was 120 bushels of fine flour and 240 bushels of meal. This detailed description gives some idea of the immense wealth of this king. There seemed to be no limit to his material resources.

Solomon had 700 wives and 300 concubines. I suppose that no one knows the number of children he had. What a host of people he had to sustain!

His stables were the largest in the world—40,000 horses for chariots and 12,000 trained horsemen (v. 26). He had more horses than any other potentate on earth. His capital city, Jerusalem, eclipsed the capitals of all other world rulers of his day. When he dedicated the great temple he had built there, he offered in one day 120,000 sheep and 22,000 oxen as dedicatory sacrifices. This is almost beyond normal comprehension.

Solomon's own palace was built of costly stones and cedar wood. Thirteen years and thousands of workmen were required for its completion. It included a tremendous and impressive armory and a hall of judgment famous throughout the world.

27

Such was the wealth of King Solomon. Few men on earth ever matched it. Human beings are prone to measure a man's greatness by the amount of wealth which he accumulates, although this is often a false measure by which to appraise a man. If greatness can be judged by the measure of wealth, King Solomon certainly was among the greatest men of all times. Yet Jesus, with sublime dignity and genuine humility, affirmed of Himself, "A greater than Solomon is here."

The Bible sets Christ forth as possessing a wealth far greater than the material wealth of King Solomon. Yet strangely, His life on earth was by no means one of wealth and luxury like that of a king but was in complete contrast to it. His birthplace was a stable. The New Testament record declares that He was born in a stable "because there was no room for them in the inn" (Luke 2:7). We may be assured that if He had been of the family of a governor or a king or a person of high estate and wealth, there would have been room in the inn. The innkeeper would not have turned away a woman about to give birth to a child and sent her to a stable if she had belonged to a wealthy or prominent family. But because Mary and Joseph were poor and common folk, there was no room for them in the inn.

Jesus was born into a common laboring family whose head and breadwinner was a lowly carpenter. He grew up in the inconspicuous little village of Nazareth and worked with his foster father, Joseph, at the carpenter's bench to earn a living. He was obviously regarded as an ordinary carpenter of the village. He said of Himself that He did not possess a place of His own on this earth to lay His head. "The foxes have holes," He commented, "and the birds of the air have nests, but the Son of man hath not where to lay His head" (Matt. 8:20). He did not hold a deed or title to any piece of property on earth so far as we know, either real estate or personal property. All He possessed was the clothing which He wore, and even this seemed to have been limited to a single outfit. Yet, in reality, He was the Lord of all. He was in the world and the world was made by Him, but the world knew Him not. Sublime is the Bible record: "Though he was rich, yet for your sakes he became poor, that ye through his poverty might be rich" (II Cor. 8:9).

We call His great acts "miracles," but to Him they were not miracles. They were simply the expression of His lordship over His own creation. For example, He was able to say to the wind and the waves, "Peace, be still" (Mark 4:39), and at His command the wind ceased and the sea became calm. He was the author of nature's so-called "laws," and He could, therefore, set these laws aside or rise above them any time He wished.

Great indeed was the true wealth of Jesus Christ. He owned all things. The world itself was His. He made it. It belonged to Him, but His emphasis during His ministry on earth was never material wealth. He knew the danger of material wealth and often warned people against the deceitfulness of riches. He knew well what wealth did to men. He saw the rich young ruler turn away from the kingdom of God because he had great riches upon which his heart was unshakingly fixed. He declared that it was easier for a camel to go through the eye of a needle than for a rich man to enter into the kingdom of heaven. He warned his listeners against laying up treasures on earth where moth and rust corrupt and thieves break through and steal. He said, "Where your treasure is, there will your heart be also" (Matt. 6:21). He exhorted people to lay up treasure in heaven rather than on earth.

Solomon was a mere man, a mere tenant of earth, while Jesus Christ is the Creator and Owner of all things. Solomon, though only a tenant of earth, lived in great luxury amid fabulous wealth. Jesus, the Creator and Owner of all, lived in simplicity and frugality. What greatness is this, and what a contrast to Solomon! Truly, a greater than Solomon existed in Jesus Christ.

The emphasis of Christ was continually upon heavenly and eternal treasures: "Therefore take no thought, saying, What shall we eat? or, What shall we drink? or, Wherewithal shall we be clothed? ... For your heavenly Father knoweth that ye have need of all these things. But seek ye first the kingdom of God, and his righteousness; and all these things shall be added unto you" (Matt. 6:31-33).

The Bible exalts and emphasizes Christ's spiritual wealth and His riches of grace. The Apostle Paul said of Him, "But my God shall supply all your need according to his riches in glory by Christ Jesus" (Phil. 4:19). All God's glorious spiritual treasures and blessings are found in Him. The Father deposited them in Him. All the riches of God's grace are bestowed upon the world in and through Jesus Christ, in whom are hid all the treasures of wisdom and knowledge and in whom alone these are to be found. The Apostle Paul declared that God had granted great grace to him in giving

30

to him the high and holy privilege of preaching "among the Gentiles the unsearchable riches of Christ" (Eph. 3:8). The riches of Christ are indeed unsearchable. They are indescribable simply because they are spiritual and eternal rather than material. The Bible continually emphasizes the riches of His glory and of His grace.

God has blessed believers in Jesus Christ with all spiritual blessings in heavenly places. That is to say, any spiritual blessing that man can seek and that God has to bestow is bestowed in and through Jesus Christ. Those who are "in Christ" become the heir of all these spiritual blessings. A study of the first chapter of Paul's Epistle to the Ephesians would be most rewarding in this connection. Jesus Christ is rich in grace, in mercy and in love.

King Solomon cannot help men today. He can do nothing to meet the needs of hearts and lives. He is dead and gone. His name is only a memory. But Jesus Christ can meet the needs of your heart right now. Do you need mercy? He is rich in mercy. Do you need grace? He is rich in grace. Do you need spiritual power? He is rich in power. Whatever any human soul may stand in need of, or deeply long for, the full provision to meet these needs and longings can be found in the infinite riches of Jesus Christ, God's eternal Son and the Saviour of men.

Chapter 4

Greater Than Solomon in Power

Jesus Christ cannot be equitably compared to any person, past or present. When He said, "A greater than Solomon is here," He was not manifesting personal conceit or arrogant egotism but was illustrating the spiritual stubbornness and blindness of the people to whom He was speaking. He was recounting the fact that the Queen of Sheba had journeyed a long distance to hear the wisdom of Solomon and said to them, "You are rejecting someone greater and more important than Solomon." Therefore, the people of her generation would rise up in indictment against the people of His own generation at the judgment day. It matters not to whom Jesus is compared, He is always greater.

We have already noted that He is greater than Solomon in wisdom, although Solomon was and is considered among the wisest of men who ever lived. And we have observed that Jesus is greater than Solomon in wealth, although Solomon was one of the wealthiest potentates that ever reigned on earth. But Solomon's wealth was only temporal and corruptible, whereas the wealth which Jesus possesses is spiritual and eternal.

Jesus is also greater than Solomon in might, or power. That Solomon was a very powerful king is beyond question in history. His power was exerted throughout the world of his day. He stood head and shoulders above most of earth's rulers so far as their power was concerned. Men universally respected and feared the strength of this great king, but in no true sense could the power of Solomon be compared to that of the Lord Jesus Christ.

Solomon had great military might. He had great political strength. He had great economic power. Beyond these few spheres, however, his power pretty much ended. Jesus, on the other hand, had no military might. He held no political position. He possessed no financial assets or economic power. And yet He affirmed a power surpassing that of King Solomon's.

First of all, Jesus Christ had power over the whole of creation, over the very decrees of nature. He commanded the wind to cease blowing and the waves of the sea to cease rolling. At His command both the wind and the waves stopped instantly, and the Sea of Galilee was calm in a matter of seconds. He simply spoke the words, "Peace, be still," and it came to pass immediately. The men marveled and said, "What manner of man is this, that even the wind and the sea obey him?" (Mark 4:41).

One day He pronounced a curse upon a fig tree that had produced leaves but no fruit. The next day the disciples observed that this fig tree was withered from the roots. He rode an unbroken colt into the city of Jerusalem, demonstrating His miraculous power over the animal kingdom.

Solomon never possessed powers of this kind, even though unfounded Jewish traditions have sought to ascribe them to him. He had his armies and navies, chariots and horsemen—soldiers in such large numbers that their maintenance was an all but unbearable burden on the people, but Solomon had no power over the wind or waves or trees or animals.

In the second place, Jesus had power over disease. He was able, by speaking but a word, to heal those plagued with the awful disease of leprosy. People who had been born blind received sight upon His touch or spoken word. Those who had been crippled for long years, some from their birth, were instantly restored. People who had never been able to stand erect, rose up instantly at His command and walked and leaped and praised God. Others who were deaf and speechless were given the power of hearing and speech at the word of Jesus. He possessed power to heal all manner of sicknesses and diseases. The sick and the afflicted flocked to Him. Some who were unable to come on their own strength were brought by relatives or friends and were instantly healed. Hundreds and perhaps thousands of people were healed by Jesus during His ministry on earth. Multitudes came to Him for healing, and they did not go away disappointed, for we read repeatedly in the four Gospels: "And he healed them all."

Solomon possessed no such power as this. Though he had his armies and navies and gold and silver and might of a kind, he had no power like this. People throughout the length and breadth of the land marveled at Jesus' deeds and said, "We never saw anything like this before!"

In the third place, Jesus had power even over demons. He commanded the demons to depart, and they obeyed Him. During the time He was on earth, demon possession was common and widespread. Such demonic possession is still common in some areas of the world and is on the increase today even in highly cultured lands. Demons are angels of the Devil, fallen angels, like Satan himself. They are able to take possession of human beings and to completely control them, sometimes making them act like maniacs. Mere men, including even those in the medical profession, do not have power over demons. But Jesus Christ needed but to speak a word, and demons departed from their victims at once. These evil beings often cried out in fear at the very sight of Him as He approached their victims. Evil spirits that had resisted all human strength and power trembled and fled at His presence and spoken word.

Satan himself, the Prince of Devils, was unable to conquer Jesus Christ, although he tried his best to do so. For 40 days and nights in the wilderness following His baptism, Jesus was tested of the Devil with every manner and form of testing possible. But He stood firm against the adversary (see Matt. 4, Luke 4). Finally, Christ conquered the Devil forever and dissipated his power by His own death on Calvary's cross (see Col. 2:14,15; Heb. 2:14,15).

Solomon did not possess such power. He himself was harrassed and overcome by Satan. A good many years of his life were lived under heavy disgrace. He became a prey to Satan's snares and pitfalls, unable to withstand his evil temptations. He fell and he fell low—a tragic victim of Satan's wiles. The very memory of King Solomon is a stumbling block to many people to this day.

In the fourth place, Jesus has power over death. He called people from the dead back to life again. One day in Galilee He encountered a funeral procession. A widow had lost her only son. She was weeping bitterly and mourning grievously. Jesus stopped the funeral procession, spoke to the corpse, and the young man sat up instantly, restored to life (Luke 7:11-15). Jairus's daughter was raised from the dead by Jesus in response to the father's earnest appeal to come and help them. Christ simply took the maiden by the hand and said, "Damsel, arise," and she arose, restored to full life and health (8:41-56). He stood at the grave of Lazarus, who had been dead and in the tomb for four days, and called out, "Lazarus, come forth!" And the dead man came walking out of the tomb, bound hand and foot in grave clothes (John 11:1-44).

Christ arose triumphantly from the grave after cruel hands had crucified Him and put Him to death. The resurrection of Christ is one of the best attested facts in history. Following His resurrection He said to His disciples: "Because I live, ye shall live also" (14:19). He conquered death itself that "he might destroy him that had the power of death, that is, the devil; and deliver them who through fear of death were all their lifetime subject to bondage" (Heb. 2:14,15). Truly, a greater than Solomon is here in the Person of Jesus Christ. He conquered death and is alive today at the right hand of the Father in heaven.

In the fifth place, Jesus Christ has power to forgive sins. In Luke 5 we have the record of Jesus speaking forgiveness to a crippled man who was brought to Him for healing. When He saw the faith of the man and of those who had brought him, He said to him, "Man, thy sins are forgiven thee"

(v. 20). The record goes on: "And the scribes and Pharisees began to reason, saying, Who is this which speaketh blasphemies? Who can forgive sins, but God alone? But when Jesus perceived their thoughts, he answering said unto them, What reason ye in your hearts? Whether is easier to say, Thy sins be forgiven thee; or to say, Rise up and walk? But that ye may know that the Son of man hath power upon earth to forgive sins, (he said unto the sick of the palsy,) I say unto thee, Arise, and take up thy couch, and go into thine house. And immediately he rose up before them, and took up that whereon he lay, and departed to his own house, glorifying God. And they were all amazed, and they glorified God, and were filled with fear, saying, We have seen strange things to day" (vv. 21-26). Their question was a legitimate one: Who can forgive sins but God alone? But Jesus proved to them that He Himself was, in fact, very deity. To prove His divine power before their eyes, He told the man to rise up and walk, and he immediately did so.

We read in Paul's Epistle to the Ephesians, "In whom we have redemption through his blood, the forgiveness of sin" (1:7), and also, that "God for Christ's sake hath forgiven you" (4:32). The power to forgive sins does not belong to human beings, but Jesus Christ possesses such power—and, thank God, He exercises it too! No one on earth holds the power to cause another person's sins to be forgiven or to affect another's relationship to God, but Jesus Christ has this power. He alone can forgive our sins and bring us into a reconciled relationship with God, a relationship which sin had broken. He alone can restore us to fellowship with

37

a holy God. Such divine power is the prerogative of deity alone, but Christ possesses it.

Who would Solomon be to pronounce divine forgiveness on sin? Who is anyone who endeavors to speak forgiveness to another person for sins which he has committed against God? True, we can forgive the sins which people have committed against us personally, but no mere human can forgive in the divine realm, in the place of God. Yet there is a Man who can do this (I Tim. 2:5,6)—the Man Christ Jesus. He has that power because He is the eternal Son of God and one with the Father.

He has power to forgive your sins, too, if you will but come to Him. He died for you, paying the penalty of your sins. If you will come to Him just as you are, He will freely and fully forgive all of your sins.

One more great fact must be mentioned. He also has power to change men's hearts and lives. He could say to the sinful woman caught in the act of adultery, "Go, and sin no more" (John 8:11). Not only was He able to forgive her sin, He was also able to change her life so that henceforth she would depart from her former shameful path to follow paths of righteousness and purity. Solomon, as the king of Israel, had it in his power to pardon any criminal in his empire, but he had no power to change that criminal's heart or nature. But Jesus Christ can do this. He not only delivers people from the penalty of sin, He also delivers them from the power of sin. This kind of power is untouched and unmatched by any human hand.

Zacchaeus, the greedy and dishonest tax collector, after he had met Jesus Christ, said, "The half of my goods I give to the poor; and if I have taken any thing from any man by false accusation, I restore him fourfold" (Luke 19:8). It requires divine power to change a greedy, selfish human heart; yet Jesus did exactly that to Zacchaeus. And He has done the same for millions of others.

Consider the great change wrought in Saul of Tarsus. This man had been one of the most vicious and determined enemies of Christ and His followers, but he was transformed by divine power to become the most devoted servant Christ has ever had. People could scarcely believe the transformation that had been wrought within him. Even Christians were suspicious of him at first, thinking he was only acting as a spy. This same man, later in life, wrote, "If any man be in Christ, he is a new creature: old things are passed away; behold, all things are become new" (II Cor. 5:17).

Jesus Christ still has this power today. He can change your heart and life and make you a new spiritual creation through the power of His glorious gospel. It is the power of God providing salvation to everyone who believes, to the Jew first and also to the Greek—and to you, and to me.

Chapter 5

Greater Than Solomon in Compassion

Jesus is really beyond comparison with any human being. The following statement, one version of "The Incomparable Christ," is true and provocative: "In infancy He startled a king; in boyhood He puzzled the doctors; in manhood He walked upon the billows and hushed the sea to sleep. He healed the multitudes without medicine and made no charge for His services. He never wrote a book, yet vast is the number of books that have been written about Him. He never wrote a song, yet He has furnished the theme of more songs than all song writers combined. He never founded a college, yet all the schools together cannot boast of as many students as He has had. Great men have come and gone, yet He lives on. Death could not destroy Him; the grave could not hold Him. Yes, Jesus Christ is beyond compare."

We have seen that Christ was greater than Solomon in wisdom, in wealth and in power. Another comparison is in order: He is greater than Solomon in compassion.

The Bible says of King Solomon, "And God gave Solomon wisdom and understanding exceeding much, and largeness of heart, even as the sand that is on the sea shore" (I Kings 4:29).

The "largeness of heart" ascribed to him here seems to indicate that there was a certain degree of compassion and mercy in the heart of King Solomon. He himself wrote some very significant things about compassion and mercy, particularly in the Book of Proverbs. For instance, he wrote: "Let not mercy and truth forsake thee: bind them upon thy neck; write them upon the table of thine heart: so shalt thou find favour and good understanding in the sight of God and man" (3:3,4). Here is good counsel to individuals to make mercy and truth a vital part of their lives and conduct, for by doing this they are assured of finding favor with both God and man. Such counsel is infallible, and the predicted results are unfailing.

In another Proverb Solomon declared, "He that despiseth his neighbour sinneth: but he that hath mercy on the poor, happy is he. Do they not err that devise evil? But mercy and truth shall be to them that devise good" (14:21,22).

Here he exhorted people not to despise others. No one is to despise his neighbor but must show him mercy. Mercy is to be shown to the poor, and happy is the one who bestows mercy upon his fellowmen. Also, this king wrote, "Mercy and truth preserve the king: and his throne is upholden by mercy" (20:28). In another place he said, "He that followeth after righteousness and mercy findeth life, righteousness, and honour" (21:21).

All of these passages show that King Solomon obviously saw the need for mercy and compassion among men; yet he did not manifest much mercy and compassion in his reign in Israel. Keeping a huge army and a powerful navy, he seemed to rule mostly by rigid might and cruel military power, and

41

these are always heartless and brutal. He ordered his personal and political adversaries put to death without mercy or leniency, regardless of who they were. Such was the case with Adonijah, a competitor to the throne (I Kings 2:23-25). Joab, who had for a time given loyalty and support to Adonijah, was snatched right from the altar in the Holy Place of the tabernacle, where he had fled for safety, and was cruelly slain on the spot (vv. 28-31). Little consideration seems to have been given to mercy under King Solomon's reign.

He also ruled by monetary force; that is, by the power of money. He levied heavy taxes on his people without sympathy and demanded heavy tribute from subdued countries without show of mercy. After Solomon's death the old men of the kingdom advised his son, the new king, saying, "Thy father made our yoke grievous: now therefore make thou the grievous service of thy father, and his heavy yoke which he put upon us, lighter, and we will serve thee" (I Kings 12:4). Unfortunately, young Reheboam "forsook the counsel of the old men, . . . and consulted with the young men, . . . [who said,] Thus shalt thou speak unto this people, . . . My little finger shall be thicker than my father's loins" (vv. 8,10). As a result the kingdom crumpled and divided. Solomon had laid an almost unbearable financial yoke upon the shoulders of his people, ruling by monetary might and economic power, which are always pitiless and harsh.

Solomon's love was a selfish kind of love, not the outreaching, self-communicating type. Whenever reference is made in the sacred record to Solomon's loving anyone, it is invariably to the baser type of love. For instance, we are told that

42

"King Solomon loved many strange women" (11:1). There is a great deal of emphasis in Scripture on his sensuous, inordinate love for women. Instead of loving a woman as his wife, as any married man of character ought to do, he loved women. In his sensuous infatuation for women he multiplied wives and concubines to a ridiculous number (1000) so that a great blot has come down through history upon his otherwise glorious name. The kind of love he had was an indictment against his character and name instead of a testimonial to him. Though Solomon surely recognized the need for genuine compassion, his own life manifested little of it.

The Bible reveals Jesus Christ preeminently as a Man of love and compassion. He had compassion on the sick. I do not know whether or not the great King Solomon's heart was moved with compassion when he saw sick people around him, but I do read repeatedly of Jesus that as He beheld the multitudes of the sick, the maimed, the halt and the blind, "He had compassion upon them . . . and healed them" (see Matt. 14:14).

Jesus possessed marked compassion for the poor and frequently consorted with them. His intimate friends and companions were from the poorer class. Though He sometimes accepted invitations into rich and wealthy homes, He usually spent His time among the common folk and championed their cause. One of the indictments He brought against the Pharisees and elders of Israel was their mistreatment and oppression of the poor. He spoke out against these practices without fear or leniency.

When people tried to silence beggars who cried

out to Him for help, He listened to the cries of the beggars rather than to the voices of those who tried to silence them. In His first public discourse in the synagogue at Nazareth, He quoted a verse from the prophecy of Isaiah: "The Lord . . . hath anointed me to preach the gospel to the poor" (Luke 4:18; see Isa. 61:1). He always had great compassion for the poor.

When John the Baptist sent from prison to find out whether or not He was indeed the Messiah, Jesus said, "Go and show John again those things which ye do hear and see: the blind receive their sight, and the lame walk, the lepers are cleansed, and the deaf hear, the dead are raised up, and the poor have the gospel preached to them" (Matt. 11:4,5).

On one occasion, while sitting opposite the temple treasury in Jerusalem watching the people cast in their money (including the rich who put in large contributions), He took special notice of the poor widow who cast in only two mites and singled her out from the rest for comment. He said, "This poor widow hath cast more in, than all they which have cast into the treasury: for all they did cast in of their abundance; but she of her want did cast in all that she had" (Mark 12:43,44).

Jesus had special compassion upon womankind. Women were generally disdained and downtrodden by the menfolk among the people of Israel in Jesus' day, and this is abundantly true in many non-Christian lands to the present day. But Jesus manifested a special concern and compassion for women. He was moved to deep sympathy for the widow of Nain who, in deep mourning, followed the bier with the body of her only son to the cemetery. Christ stopped the funeral procession and with His miraculous power restored the lad to life. The Lord did this because He had compassion upon the bereaved, widowed mother.

When a sinful woman taken in the act of adultery was brought to Him by the Pharisees, He showed compassion and forgave her sins. Not only did He forgive her sins, but He gave her power to go forth into a life of purity and uprightness, to sin no more.

Though the woman of Samaria who came to Jacob's well to draw water was obviously a woman of disrepute among her own people, Jesus had compassion upon her. He knew that her life of sin had not satisfied her inner longings, and His great heart of love went out to her. Engaging her in conversation, He gradually revealed Himself to her as her Messiah, Saviour and Deliverer.

He sharply rebuked the scribes and Pharisees for their heartless mistreatment of women, especially of helpless widows. Stronger language than He used against these men can scarcely be conceived: "Woe unto you, scribes and Pharisees, hypocrites! for ye devour widows' houses, and for a pretence make long prayer: therefore ye shall receive the greater damnation" (Matt. 23:14).

There was the time when Mary of Bethany broke the alabaster box of costly ointment and poured its contents on His head in the house of Simon the leper. Her action drew from Him this comment when some criticized her for the waste: "Let her alone; why trouble ye her? She hath wrought a good work on me. . . . She hath done what she could. . . . Verily I say unto you, Wheresoever this gospel shall be preached throughout the whole world, this also that she hath done shall be spoken of for a memorial of her" (Mark 14:6,8,9; see John 12:1-8).

On another occasion when a woman of ill fame came into the house of Jesus' rich host, Simon the Pharisee, and washed His feet with her tears and wiped them with her hair, this, too, brought criticism. The critics said, "This man, if he were a prophet, would have known who and what manner of woman this is that toucheth him: for she is a sinner" (Luke 7:39). Jesus showed that though this woman had been a great sinner, she was expressing to Him the gratitude and joy she had found in forgiveness and cleansing.

The parable which Jesus told about the creditor with the two debtors brought the application that the one who has been forgiven much loves much and the one who has been forgiven little loves little. The parable was given in defense of the woman.

Jesus also manifested a very deep and special love for children. They flocked to Him wherever He was. It has been said by some that though Jesus wept several times, it is never recorded of Him that He smiled or laughed. However, we are not to conclude from this silence that He did not smile or laugh. The fact that children loved Him and flocked to Him would strongly indicate that He did smile and laugh, for children are never drawn to sad and gloomy people. He took little children up in His arms and blessed them. When the disciples rebuked the people who brought the little ones, feeling He should not be bothered by them, He said, "Suffer little children, and forbid them not, to come unto me: for of such is the kingdom of heaven" (Matt. 19:14).

Above all He had great compassion and love for penitent sinners. Though He had an unchangeable hatred for sin, He had an unquenchable love for sinners. All sin-laden ones who came to Him with a true spirit of repentance and desire for pardon received freely from Him. He never failed to show compassion to them. He had no compassion on hypocrites who pretended to be what they were not; but for those who recognized their sins and confessed them, He always manifested limitless love and a deep desire to help them. The attitude of His heart is made clear in His own words: "They that be whole need not a physician, but they that are sick. . . . I am not come to call the righteous, but sinners to repentance" (9:12,13).

The self-righteous and hypocritical Pharisees received from Him the harshest rebukes and indictments that could come from lips of flesh and blood; but the poor and lowly, though laden with sin and iniquity, drew from His lips words of pardon and love upon confession and repentance.

It was because of His love that He came into the world in the first place to be the Saviour of men. It was because of His love for sinners that He went to the cross to die for them. The divine testimonial to this is: "Having loved his own which were in the world, he loved them unto the end" (John 13:1). Another is: "Christ also hath loved us, and hath given himself for us an offering and a sacrifice to God" (Eph. 5:2); and, "God . . . loved me, and gave himself for me" (Gal. 2:20). He who loved men enough to go to the cross bearing their sins loves us enough still to receive with joy and

gladness all who will come to God by Him in repentance and faith.

Chapter 6

Greater Than Solomon in Glory

There was much glory attached to Solomon's kingdom. His reign is known as the "Golden Age" of the Kingdom of Israel. His fame and glory were widespread. Any reference to the glory of King Solomon was bound to find a responsive chord in the hearts of Jewish people of Jesus' generation—a response that extends even to the present generation.

Jesus made good use of this fact to teach an important spiritual lesson when He said, "Consider the lilies of the field, how they grow; . . . yet I say unto you, That even Solomon in all his glory was not arrayed like one of these" (Matt. 6:28,29). The reason He referred to the glory of Solomon was that the people knew much about this and it carried great weight in their minds. Any emphasis on the glory of Solomon and his reign could not fail to attract their ears. Though the lilies of the field neither toil nor spin, they exceeded "even Solomon in all his glory" (v. 29) in their beauty and array. This wonderfully emphasizes the glory of the Heavenly Father in His care for His children! In the text we have been considering, "A greater than Solomon is here" (12:42), a tremendous impact was made upon the minds of Jesus' hearers. The comparison could not escape their notice even though it might have angered and embittered them.

Solomon's gilt-edged reputation had reached far and wide, even to the distant land of the Queen of Sheba. She could hardly believe all the fantastic things that she had been told about this man, so she journeyed all the way to Jerusalem to see and to find out for herself. When she arrived and saw all of Solomon's glory, she was overwhelmed and astounded and exclaimed, "Behold, the half was not told me!" (I Kings 10:7).

Much glory was attached to Solomon, both to his majestic person and to his remarkable kingdom. He lacked nothing that could contribute to earthly glory, and he spared nothing to make his reign illustrious. His private palace was likely the most glorious mansion known at that time. His banquet hall awed all who were invited to feast in it. His retinue of soldiers and servants exceeded that of any other living potentate. His fabulous wealth earned him a great reputation in temporal glory. The costly robes he wore and the luxurious uniforms worn by his servants and officers all contributed to the glory and fame of this great king. The temple he built in Jerusalem for the worship of the Lord was known throughout the world and surpassed every other structure in glory. But compared to the glory of our Lord Jesus Christ, all the glory of Solomon pales into insignificance.

Christ's glory not only far exceeds that of Solomon but also is of an entirely different kind. Solomon's glory was terrestrial and temporal; the glory of Jesus Christ is celestial and eternal. Notice Paul's comment about these two kinds of glory in I Corinthians 15:40. Jesus is designated by two inspired apostles in the New Testament as the very

"Lord of glory" (I Cor. 2:8; James 2:1). Where does this put Solomon? The Apostle Paul praises and amplifies the "glory of his [Christ's] grace" and "the riches of the glory of his inheritance in the saints" (Eph. 1:6,18). Who could imagine such things being said about Solomon?

In much the same strain the Apostle John wrote: "The Word [Christ] was made flesh, and dwelt among us, (and we beheld his glory, the glory as of the only begotten of the Father,) full of grace and truth. . . . And of his fulness have all we received, and grace for grace" (John 1:14,16).

The Apostle Peter testified that God "raised him [Christ] up from the dead, and gave him glory; that your faith and hope might be in God" (I Pet. 1:21). Resurrection glory! Such glory belonged not to Solomon nor indeed to any other human. It is the resurrection glory that is referred to as "the glory of the celestial" in I Corinthians 15:40. The glory of Jesus' resurrection from the dead so far outshines any human glory that no real comparison is possible.

Peter testified, "All flesh is as grass, and all the glory of man as the flower of grass. The grass withereth, and the flower thereof falleth away" (I Pet. 1:24). This is the only kind of glory Solomon possessed. How different from the resurrection glory of the Lord of Life, Jesus Christ!

The writer of the Epistle to the Hebrews said of Christ, "This man was counted worthy of more glory than Moses, inasmuch as he who hath builded the house hath more honour than the house" (3:3). Few men shine forth more gloriously in Jewish history than Moses and Solomon, yet the Bible declares that Jesus is greater and worthy of more glory than both of these.

I think the most astounding statement in all of the Scriptures about the glory of Jesus Christ is found in Hebrews 1: "Who being the brightness of his glory, and the express image of his person, and upholding all things by the word of his power, when he had by himself purged our sins, sat down on the right hand of the Majesty on high" (v. 3). The New American Standard Bible gives this translation: "He is the radiance of His glory and the exact representation of His nature, and upholds all things by the word of His power. When He had made purification of sins, He sat down at the right hand of the Majesty on high." Who could imagine such a description coming from any source, human or divine, about King Solomon? Well indeed did Jesus say of Himself, "A greater than Solomon is here."

When Jesus was born in Bethlehem, a special, brilliant star appeared in the sky to indicate the time and place of His birth. Wise men from the East, astronomers, followed the star until it led them to the place where they found Him. Outside the city of Bethlehem on a hillside, "the angel of the Lord came upon them [shepherds], and the glory of the Lord shone round about them: and they were sore afraid. And the angel said unto them, Fear not: for, behold, I bring you good tidings of great joy, which shall be to all people. For unto you is born this day in the city of David a Saviour, which is Christ the Lord. . . . And suddenly there was with the angel a multitude of the heavenly host praising God, and saying, Glory to God in the highest, and on earth peace, good will toward men" (Luke 2:9-11,13,14). No such glorious phenomena attended the birth of Solomon nor that of any other man.

At Christ's baptism the heavens opened, the Spirit of God "like a dove" lighted upon Him, while a voice from heaven spoke, saying, "This is my beloved Son, in whom I am well pleased" (Matt. 3:16,17).

At His word the blind were made to see, the lame walked and the lepers were healed. Such was the glory of Jesus. When people, even His enemies, listened to Him, they said, "Never man spake like this man" (John 7:46). When many saw His miracles, they testified, "We never saw it on this fashion" (Mark 2:12).

On Mount Hermon He was transfigured before the eyes of His disciples into a figure of dazzling heavenly glory. Referring to this experience many years later, Simon Peter wrote, "We . . . were eyewitnesses of his majesty. For he received from God the Father honour and glory, when there came such a voice to him from the excellent glory, This is my beloved Son, in whom I am well pleased. And this voice which came from heaven we heard, when we were with him in the holy mount" (II Pet. 1:16-18).

During most of the time Jesus was upon earth He had to conceal His true glory, but on a few occasions it broke through in its divine brilliance, and people were awed and amazed. One such occasion was in the Garden of Gethsemane. When His enemies came to arrest Him, they fell backward upon the ground in paralytic fear (John 18:6). At Calvary when He was crucified, the earth trembled, rocks were split and the veil in the Jerusalem temple was torn from top to bottom. Even the sun withheld its light in the face of the dying Lamb of God (Matt. 27:45-53). All of these phenomena give us glimpses of the glory of the Son of Man.

In His own prayer to the Father recorded in John 17, our Lord lifted up His eyes to heaven and said, "Father, the hour is come; glorify thy Son, that thy Son also may glorify thee. . . . O Father, glorify thou me with thine own self with the glory which I had with thee before the world was" (vv. 1,5).

His glory was not merely a celestial glory but also an eternal glory. He has shared the glory of His Father since the beginningless ages of eternity. This was His real glory, the glory which had to be largely veiled during His incarnation upon earth.

As we have already intimated, the greatest glory of all, the climax of His glory on this earth, was that of His resurrection. An earthquake shook the land, an angel rolled back the stone which sealed His tomb, and He came forth alive. Two angels appeared in shining garments at the entrance, and with a kind of heavenly irony they asked the seekers who came to the tomb, "Why seek ye the living among the dead?" (Luke 24:5). Then the angels added, "He is not here, but is risen" (v. 6). He had been raised from the dead by divine power.

When the weeping Mary recognized Him as her risen Lord, she cried out, "Rabboni," meaning "My Master, or, My Lord" (John 20:16). Doubting Thomas, when he saw with his own eyes and felt with his own hands the risen body of Jesus, cried, "My Lord and my God!" (v. 28). This is the glory of His resurrection!

The disciples' jeopardy was turned to joy when they saw their Lord risen from the dead. Their fear was changed to faith, their doubts were turned to belief, their despair gave way to new hope, their cowardice turned to courage, and their confusion became new devotion. There could be no doubt about Him now, no more uncertainty, no more despair, no more fear. Jesus Christ was indeed the Messiah and the Son of God—He was risen from the dead! They beheld Him in resurrection glory. They saw, heard and felt Him. He entered closed rooms and walked upon the waters of the sea.

Following His resurrection He made an appointment with His disciples to meet them on a mountain in Galilee. There He said to them, "All power is given unto me in heaven and in earth. Go ye therefore, and teach all nations, baptizing them in the name of the Father, and of the Son, and of the Holy Ghost: teaching them to observe all things whatsoever I have commanded you: and, lo, I am with you alway, even unto the end of the world" (Matt. 28:18-20).

Forty days after He had come out of the tomb, He led them all out to the Mount of Olives. After once more commissioning them to be witnesses to Him in Jerusalem, in Judea and in Samaria and to the uttermost part of the earth, He was taken up, and a cloud received Him out of their sight (Acts 1:8,9). It was a glorious sight the disciples saw as He disappeared into heavenly glory. Then two angels appeared who said, "Ye men of Galilee, why stand ye gazing up into heaven? This same Jesus, which is taken up from you into heaven, shall so come in like manner as ye have seen him go into heaven" (v. 11).

The glory of Jesus Christ is greater than Solomon's indeed! No man in the realm of human history was ever granted resurrection glory. Solomon's body and bones have long ago decayed, and not even a tomb remains holding his dust. So it is with Abraham, Jacob, Joseph, Moses, Job, Samuel, David, Isaiah, Daniel—their bodies have all gone to corruption, they have returned to the earth. The same is true of all great religious leaders of the world: Confucius, Buddha, Zoroaster, Muhammad—these are all dead and their bodies have returned to corruption. But Jesus Christ is alive! He left behind Him an open, empty grave. He came forth from it triumphant over the power of death in the glory of His Heavenly Father, which He had before the world began.

He has been received back again into glory and is seated at the right hand of the Majesty on high. He is there at the throne of God making intercession for all who will come unto God by Him. "When he had by himself purged our sins, [He] sat down on the right hand of the Majesty on high" (Heb. 1:3). "Seeing then that we have a great high priest, that is passed into the heavens, Jesus the Son of God, let us hold fast our profession. For we have not an high priest which cannot be touched with the feeling of our infirmities; but was in all points tempted like as we are, yet without sin. Let us therefore come boldly unto the throne of grace, that we may obtain mercy, and find grace to help in time of need" (4:14-16).

In His Sermon on the Mount, Jesus declared that the glory of the lilies of the field exceeded the glory of Solomon, yet in many respects it was the same kind of glory. The flower of the grass falls to

56

the ground and withers; Solomon's glory became sadly tainted and was short lived. The glory of Jesus Christ exceeds that of Solomon and all the kings, leaders, teachers and prophets of all history. His is untainted glory—pure, divine, everlasting.

The most wonderful thing of all about the glory of Jesus Christ is that He wants us to share it with Him. Even in this life after we have been reconciled to Him and walk in His fellowship, we see "the glory of God in the face of Jesus Christ" (II Cor. 4:6). Besides this, as we with open face behold as "in a glass the glory of the Lord, [we] are changed into the same image from glory to glory, even as by the Spirit of the Lord" (3:18).

The Apostle Paul described salvation as being "in Christ Jesus with eternal glory" (II Tim. 2:10). Peter called himself "a witness of the sufferings of Christ, and also a partaker of the glory that shall be revealed" (I Pet. 5:1).

All believers will someday share the personal glory of Jesus Christ for ever and ever. Paul wrote to the Thessalonian Christians: "He called you by our gospel, to the obtaining of the glory of our Lord Jesus Christ" (II Thess. 2:14). In his Epistle to the Colossians he declared, "When Christ, who is our life, shall appear, then shall ye also appear with him in glory" (3:4). When Christ thus comes to receive His own to Himself, He will "change our vile body, that it may be fashioned like unto his glorious body, according to the working whereby he is able even to subdue all things unto himself" (Phil. 3:21).

In his great classic passage about present life and future glory, the Apostle Paul wrote: "For our light affliction, which is but for a moment, work-

eth for us a far more exceeding and eternal weight
of glory; while we look not at the things which are
seen, but at the things which are not seen: for the
things which are seen are temporal; but the things
which are not seen are eternal'' (II Cor. 4:17,18).

All who put their trust in Him and follow Him
are being gradually transformed into His image,
from glory to glory, day by day even in this present life. And some day when He comes again to
receive His own, they will be made utterly like Him
to share His glory for ever and ever.

Chapter 7

A Greater Temple Than Solomon's

One special thing for which King Solomon was particularly renowned was the great temple which he built in the city of Jerusalem. This was one of the most famed achievements of his reign. But Christ is greater than Solomon in that He is building a temple of more grandeur and higher importance than the one built by Solomon. In order to get the full impact of this contrast, we need to recollect the greatness and the grandeur of Solomon's temple.

Solomon was chosen of God to build the temple. His father, King David, had wanted to build a temple for Jehovah; but because he had been so much a man of war and bloodshed, God would not allow him to do so. God decreed, instead, that Solomon should do it. David, however, prepared and stored up a great deal of material for the erection of the temple, especially gold and silver, to aid in having his desire carried out by his son.

For the building of the temple Solomon gathered material and workmen from many lands, particularly from Tyre, a great country of arts, crafts and commerce. He bargained with Tyre's King Hiram to supply him with sufficient cedar for the temple as well as other special building materials.

The temple was 60 cubits long (about 90 ft., or

27.5 m.), 20 cubits wide (about 30 ft., or 9.1 m.) and 30 cubits high (about 45 ft., or 13.7 m.). The massive walls were of stone expertly cut at the quarries. When the pieces were brought together at the temple site, they fitted so perfectly that no sound of hammer or chisel was heard in the building. Though the basic structure of the temple was principally of stone, it was completely lined with cedar boards, and the entire interior was then overlaid with gold. At the main entrance on the east were two huge pillars of pure bronze, and these were of international distinction and fame.

Ten lamps of solid gold lighted the main sanctuary. "So Solomon overlaid the house within with pure gold: and he made a partition by the chains of gold before the oracle; and he overlaid it with gold. And the whole house he overlaid with gold, until he had finished all the house: also the whole altar that was by the oracle he overlaid with gold" (I Kings 6:21,22). "And the candlesticks of pure gold, five on the right side, and five on the left, before the oracle, with the flowers, and the lamps, and the tongs of gold, and the bowls, and the snuffers, and the basons, and the spoons, and the censers of pure gold; and the hinges of gold, both for the doors of the inner house, the most holy place, and for the doors of the house, to wit, of the temple" (7:49,50).

The great oracle in the inner sanctuary was also overlaid with pure gold, as was the table of showbread and the altar of incense. Gracing the great temple court were ten huge lavers of solid brass for the use of the priests in performing their various washings and the cleansing of the various sacrifices and instruments of service. In addition to these ten separate lavers, Hiram, a man of Tyre who was a craftsman in metals, "made a molten [brass] sea, ten cubits [about 15 ft., or 4.6 m.] from the one brim to the other: it was round all about, and his height was five cubits [about 7.5 ft., or 2.3 m.]. . . . It stood upon twelve oxen, three looking toward the north, and three looking toward the west, and three looking toward the south and three looking toward the east: and the sea was set above upon them. . . . And it was an hand breadth thick, and the brim thereof was wrought like the brim of a cup, with flowers of lilies: it contained two thousand baths [approximately 10,000 gallons, or 38,000 liters]" (I Kings 7:23,25,26).

The great brazen altar for sacrifice which stood in front of the temple was the object of wonder and the topic of conversation throughout the world. "Twenty cubits the length thereof, and twenty cubits the breadth thereof, and ten cubits the height thereof" (II Chron. 4:1). The standard cubit in the days of Israel's kings was equal to about 18 inches. This would make the altar about 30 feet long (9.1 m.), about 30 feet wide (9.1 m.) and about 15 feet high (4.6 m.).

One is awed by the description of the grandeur of this temple and its equally magnificent furniture and accessories. It is not surprising that it was considered one of the wonders of the world! But great and grand though Solomon's temple was, the temple which Jesus Christ is building today is greater and more glorious.

One day in Jerusalem some people called Jesus' attention to the great temple and its related structures, but He said to them, "See ye not all these things? Verily I say unto you, There shall not be

61

left here one stone upon another, that shall not be thrown down" (Matt. 24:2).

This was true of Solomon's temple, as it also became true of Herod's temple. So it is ultimately with all the material enterprises of men upon the earth. Change and decay is the fate of every material structure upon the face of the earth, past and present.

What kind of temple is Jesus Christ building which exceeds all the glory of Solomon's temple? For the answer to this we must go to the New Testament. In the Epistle of Paul to the Ephesian Christians we have this statement: "Now therefore ye are no more strangers and foreigners, but fellow-citizens with the saints, and of the household of God; and are built upon the foundation of the apostles and prophets, Jesus Christ himself being the chief corner stone; in whom all the building fitly framed together groweth unto an holy temple in the Lord: in whom ye also are builded together for an habitation of God through the Spirit" (Eph. 2:19-22).

Before conversion to Christ, these Ephesians were Gentile heathen, but now in Christ they were no longer strangers and foreigners to God. They were fellow citizens with the saints, members of the family of God and constituted a spiritual "house" built upon the foundation of the apostles and prophets, with Jesus Christ Himself as the chief cornerstone.

This whole spiritual building is fitly framed together, forming a holy temple for the Lord. Paul was saying to them, in essence, "You people who have been saved and regenerated by the gospel of Jesus Christ have been formed together in a building, founded upon the apostles and prophets, with Jesus Christ as the cornerstone—a temple in which God will dwell in the Person of the Holy Spirit."

Simon Peter added further to this picture in his first epistle by saying, "Ye also, as lively stones, are built up a spiritual house, an holy priesthood, to offer up spiritual sacrifices, acceptable to God by Jesus Christ. Wherefore also it is contained in the scripture, Behold, I lay in Sion a chief corner stone, elect, precious: and he that believeth on him shall not be confounded" (I Pet. 2:5,6).

Paraphrasing again, I believe he was saying, "You have been formed into a spiritual priesthood and have been built into a spiritual temple. You are individually all living stones, each being a part of the spiritual temple which Jesus Christ is building for His Heavenly Father."

In the third chapter of the Book of Hebrews we read of Christ "as a son over his own house" (v. 6). Here it is stated that Moses was faithful to God in all his house as a servant, but Christ as a son over His own house, "whose house are we, if we hold fast the confidence and the rejoicing of the hope firm unto the end" (v. 6). Again it is seen that the house or temple of Christ is constituted of His redeemed people. All who have been redeemed by Him have been formed together into a spiritual house, or temple, which He as the Redeemer is building in the world.

The Prophet Isaiah seems to have had a foreview of this when he made the statement "Thus saith the high and lofty One that inhabiteth eternity, whose name is Holy; I dwell in the high and holy place, with him also that is of a contrite and humble spirit" (Isa. 57:15). Though God is the high and lofty One who inhabits eternity, He will dwell with a man who is of a contrite spirit; that is, He is willing to take up His abode in the sanctified spirits of those who have accepted His redeeming grace.

The Apostle Paul, speaking to the heathen philosophers of Athens, declared, "God that made the world and all things therein, seeing that he is Lord of heaven and earth, dwelleth not in temples made with hands; neither is worshipped with men's hands, as though he needed any thing, seeing he giveth to all life, and breath, and all things" (Acts 17:24,25).

Here again the idea is touched upon that God does not dwell in material temples. Though He did see fit to make the temple in Jerusalem His temporary dwelling place, His house upon earth so to speak, His real dwelling place is not in a building erected by men's hands. It is a spiritual temple which He is building, one not made with human hands. It is formed of "living stones," individual men and women who have been redeemed by His grace from the various peoples of the earth and placed together into the Church. This is the true spiritual house which God has ordained for Himself.

Like a wise master builder He hews us from rough, hard rocks, digs us from the slimy pits of sin and fits us together as "living stones" in His own spiritual temple. He shapes us, cleanses us, polishes us and fits us together. He is gathering these living stones for His house from among all the nations of the earth through the proclamation of the gospel to all men.

This holy house can be completed only

through worldwide evangelization. This was the reason for Christ's great commission to His disciples to go into all the world and preach the gospel to every creature. We are His workmen to help gather out the "living stones" from every land of earth, "stones" which God puts into place in His house. And then the headstone of the corner Himself will appear to complete the holy edifice.

This is the temple which Jesus Christ is building. In common biblical phraseology, this is "His Church." The word, of course, does not merely designate a certain denomination or even a certain building, but signifies the true spiritual house, the true Body of Jesus Christ, made up of "living stones" gathered from among the nations.

The redeemed men and women who constitute these "living stones" are to be from all races and classes, and His omnipotent grace and power gloriously fits them together to form the house of God. This is the spiritual temple which the Lord Jesus Christ is in the process of building—a temple more glorious than Solomon's!

The Apostle Paul wrote: "We are labourers together with God: ye are God's husbandry, ye are God's building. According to the grace of God which is given unto me, as a wise masterbuilder, I have laid the foundation, and another buildeth thereon. But let every man take heed how he buildeth thereupon. For other foundation can no man lay than that is laid, which is Jesus Christ" (I Cor. 3:9-11).

Chapter 8

Greater Influence Than Solomon's

In contrasting the greatness of Solomon with that of Jesus Christ, we saw in our last study that the Lord is building a temple greater than the one Solomon built in Jerusalem. Christ's is a spiritual temple, the Church, and it is being constructed of "living stones" (see I Pet. 2:4)—men and women saved by His grace out of every kindred, tongue, people and nation upon the face of the earth (see Rev. 5:9).

In closing our study we shall observe that Jesus exerted a far greater influence in the world than Solomon ever did and that He is far greater than Solomon in influence.

It cannot be denied that Solomon was a man of great and far-reaching influence. This was the very reason the Queen of Sheba came to visit him. His influence had extended throughout the earth to her distant empire. She had heard much about him and had been influenced by what she had heard. Kings, princes and political leaders throughout the earth knew about Solomon and talked about him. He exerted great influence near and far.

His influence did not entirely terminate upon his death, as is the case with most people. The life and exploits of Solomon have lived on through the centuries and still exert an influence in the world. His Books of Proverbs, Ecclesiastes and the Song of

Solomon are still influencing the lives of millions. His unique reputation and name have been a strong influence among the Jewish people of the world to the present time. His name is also known and honored among the vast multitude of Muslims and still influences them. The powerful Masonic Lodge derives many of its traditions and practices from King Solomon by their own confession. His influence on history profoundly affects the great historians of the world. Solomon still exerts a very positive influence in vast areas of our world today, but compared to the influence of Jesus Christ it is pale and trivial.

Though Jesus Christ was born in a stable in the little town of Bethlehem among a comparatively insignificant people, He has changed the entire course of history by His influence. The world dates calendars from His birth: "A.D. 2000" signifies *"Anno Domini*, or Year of our Lord, 2000." History prior to the time of Christ is denoted "B.C.," "Before Christ."

His influence upon the entire world is unequalled. He never wrote a book, He never founded a school, He never had a lecture hall, He was not featured on any popular rostrum, He never launched an organization. He never erected a single building, and yet His Church today is virtually universal and has permeated every area of the world.

Millions acclaim their faith in Him. No doubt there are hundreds of thousands, even millions, of people in the world today who would gladly die for Christ if they had to. Millions have done so throughout history, even in our own generation. Some place their lives in constant jeopardy by speaking of their faith in Him as their Saviour and

Lord without hesitation or restraint, willing both to suffer and to die for Him if need be.

The preaching of Christ's gospel has changed the entire course of nations. They have been turned from darkness to light as a result of the proclamation and power of His glorious gospel. This works in reverse too. Some nations which once had His gospel and adhered to it have turned their backs on Him and have plunged into social, moral and spiritual darkness and the most crude and cruel barbarianism. Communism and Nazism are modern examples of this.

Jesus Christ has transformed whole societies. His gospel has done more to abolish slavery than anything else in the world. It has done more to elevate women to a high plane than any other influence or organization on earth. His servants have done more to alleviate pain and suffering and to promote human love and sympathy than all other agencies and organizations put together. He has had a tremendous influence in the world—and He still has.

Not only does Christ have the power and influence to achieve transformation of conditions and circumstances, but above all He is also able to change and transform the individual lives and characters of men. John Newton, the profligate and degenerate British sailor, became one of the godly clergymen of England whose ministry and influence in turn transformed other thousands.

John Bunyan, the corrupt tinker of Bedford, England, used language so foul that even ungodly mothers drew their children off the streets when he came by lest they should hear his vile speech and imitate his vocabulary. Yet he became the author of a great Christian classic of the English language, *Pilgrim's Progress*. This book, in turn, has been used of God to transform hundreds of thousands, possibly millions, of lives. Count Nikolaus von Zinzendorf, a wealthy German nobleman of the early eighteenth century, came to know Jesus Christ as his Lord and Saviour, renounced all his wealth and luxury for His sake and became a self-sacrificing and influential missionary. Out of his work came the Moravian Church and the great Moravian Missionary Society.

When missionary Robert Moffat went to South Africa, the mere mention of the name of a certain wicked pagan chief, Africaner, caused people in neighboring tribes to fear and tremble. Later Moffat brought this wicked man to a saving knowledge of Christ, and he became a sweet and meek Christian disciple and a man of far-reaching Christian influence among the peoples of South Africa. Such is the power and influence of Jesus Christ.

Alcoholics, dope addicts, criminals and degenerates of all kinds have been transformed by faith in Jesus Christ. This work still goes on around the world in individual lives, in communities and in nations. The gospel is the power of God for the salvation of everyone who believes, and this is being proved the world around every day, every month and every year.

What about you? Do you know this power in your life? Do you know the Saviour who can change your life, your home, your circumstances and your destiny? Put your faith in Him who is not only greater than Solomon but greater than any and all else in the world—past or present—Jesus

Christ, the same yesterday, today and forever. "To day if ye will hear his voice, harden not your hearts" (Heb. 4:7).